This book belongs to:

_____

Draw a self-portrait.

5 7 9 10 8 6

Ebury Press, an imprint of Ebury Publishing
20 Vauxhall Bridge Road
London SW1V 2SA

Ebury Press is part of the Penguin Random House group of companies
whose addresses can be found at global.penguinrandomhouse.com

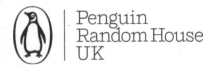

Penguin
Random House
UK

Font LSTK Bembo by studioelastik.com

First published by Ebury Press in 2016
www.eburypublishing.co.uk

A CIP catalogue record for this book is available from the British Library

ISBN 9781785032950

Illustrated by Tilly aka Running For Crayons

Printed and bound in Great Britain by Clays Ltd, Elcograf S.p.A

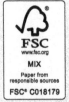

Penguin Random House is committed to a
sustainable future for our business, our readers
and our planet. This book is made from Forest
Stewardship Council® certified paper.

FSC
www.fsc.org
MIX
Paper from
responsible sources
FSC® C018179

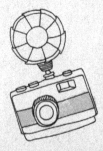

DRAW MY LIFE

This book is your chance to chart the most important events in your life so far, as well as the stupid ones, the embarrassing ones, and the ones that make you feel a little teary. So dig out your best colouring pencils and get to work, using the prompts on each page to unlock every memory stored somewhere in your head, and create a lasting record of your life that you can treasure forever.

Draw a picture of
you as a baby.

WRITE DOWN THE STORY OF YOUR BIRTH. (UNLESS YOU HAVE AN AMAZING MEMORY, YOU MIGHT HAVE TO ASK SOMEONE.)

_____

_____

_____

_____

_____

_____

_____

_____

_____

_____

_____

_____

_____

_____

_____

_____

_____

_____

Draw something important that happened the year you were born (other than your super-important entry to the world).

Write it down like this is a history book.

Draw a picture of everyone you think of as your family.

LIST THEIR NAMES HERE.

Illustrate your very earliest memory, even if it's seriously foggy.

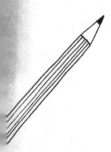

Explain what's going on.

Redraw your parents' favourite photo of you as a child – drool and all.

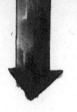

What's happening in it?

Dig out the toy you used to take EVERYWHERE from wherever it's gathering dust. Draw it here, then sleep with it every day for a week to make it feel loved.

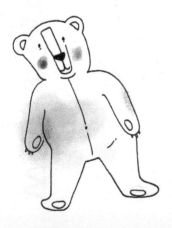

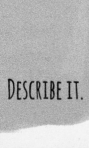

DESCRIBE IT.

Draw yourself in your uniform on your very first day of school.

What can you remember?

DRAW YOUR FACE THAT TIME
YOU CALLED **YOUR TEACHER MUM.**

OR SOMETHING EQUALLY EMBARRASSING...

Tell the story! (This book is for your eyes only!)

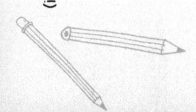

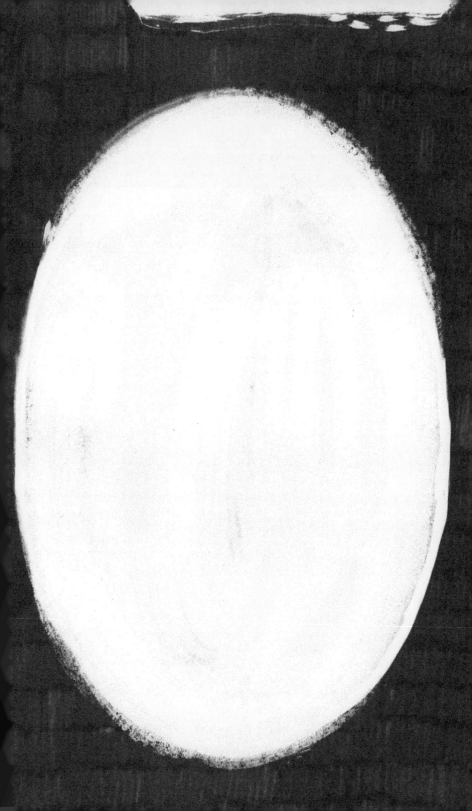

Draw the moment you learnt something BIG, like how to swim or ride a bike.

Did you think you
were the dog's tuxedo?

Draw your first
class photo.

LIST ALL THE NAMES OF YOUR CLASSMATES
(THAT YOU CAN REMEMBER).

_____   _____

_____   _____

_____   _____

_____   _____

_____   _____

_____   _____

_____   _____

_____   _____

_____   _____

_____   _____

_____   _____

_____   _____

DRAW YOUR FAVOURITE BIRTHDAY PARTY EVER.

Describe it!
What you wore,
what you ate, what
music you listened
to - everything.

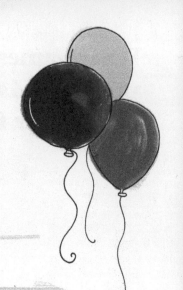

_____

_____

_____

_____

_____

_____

_____

_____

_____

_____

_____

What games did you play with your friends in the playground? Draw your fave.

The rules:

Draw a map of your neighbourhood

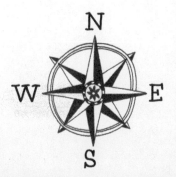

Draw the story
that your family
reminisces about
most often.

WRITE IT IN THE STYLE OF THE PERSON WHO USUALLY TELLS IT.

_____

_____

_____

_____

_____

_____

_____

_____

_____

_____

_____

_____

_____

_____

_____

_____

_____

Draw the cover of your favourite book when you were little.

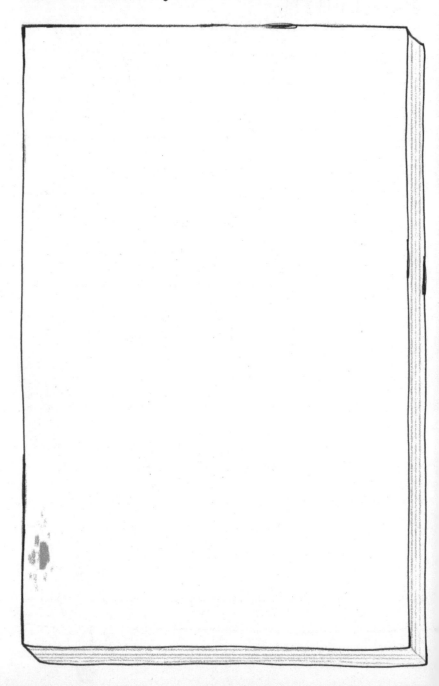

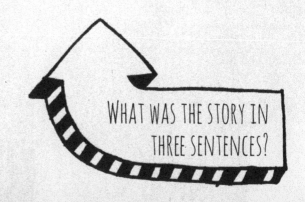

WHAT WAS THE STORY IN THREE SENTENCES?

Did you ever get lost when you were young? Perhaps on purpose to freak your mum out? Draw the scene.

TELL THE TALE.

DRAW YOUR HERO GROWING UP.
HOW COME YOU LOOKED UP TO THEM?

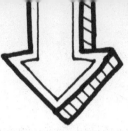

Draw your hero now.
Why them?

Draw the sleepover you remember best.

Z Z Z Z Z Z z

What did you get up to? What secrets did you tell?

If you have siblings, get
them to dip their finger
in paint and print it
here. (If they argue, do
it while they're asleep.)

Write your favourite thing about each of them.

_____

_____

_____

_____

_____

_____

_____

_____

_____

_____

_____

_____

_____

What did you buy with your pocket money when you were little?

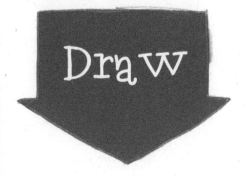

Draw your
family holiday
survival kit.

WRITE EVERYTHING YOU WOULD TAKE HERE.

Draw the best family holiday you've ever been on.

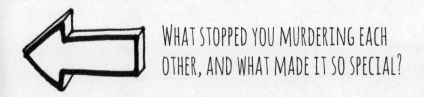

WHAT STOPPED YOU MURDERING EACH OTHER, AND WHAT MADE IT SO SPECIAL?

Draw a picture of your favourite pet - Cuddles? Deputy Dawg? Sir Barks-A-Lot?

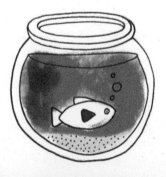

WHAT'S YOUR FAVOURITE MEMORY OF THEM?

DRAW THE WORST ARGUMENT YOU'VE
EVER HAD WITH ANYONE.

Did you win?

Draw the thing that made
you laugh so hard a bit
of wee came out.

Describe it here.

DRAW YOUR FAVOURITE SNACK WHEN YOU WERE IN PRIMARY SCHOOL...

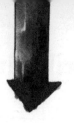

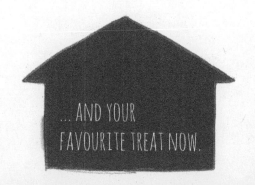
... AND YOUR
FAVOURITE TREAT NOW.

If you have a little brother or sister, draw you meeting them for the first time.

WERE YOU PROUD OR DID YOU PLOT TO GET RID OF THEM?

WHAT WAS YOUR DREAM JOB WHEN YOU WERE LITTLE?
DRAW YOURSELF IN THAT CAREER.

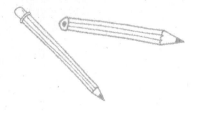

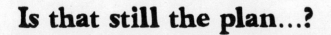

Is that still the plan...?

Draw your favourite memory from secondary school.

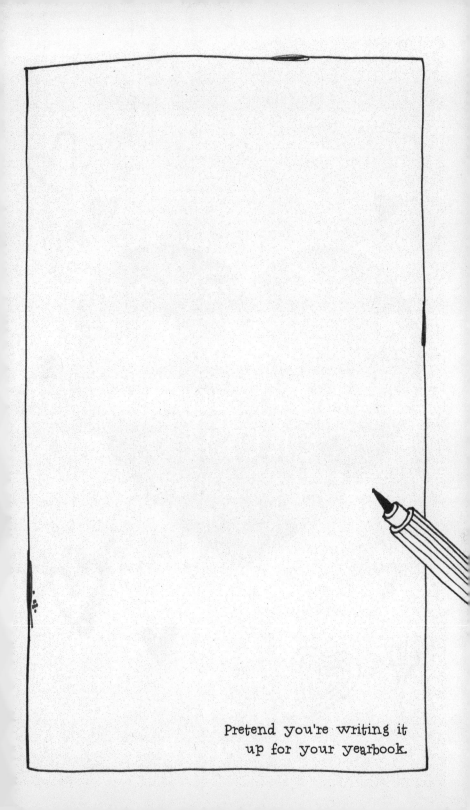

Pretend you're writing it
up for your yearbook.

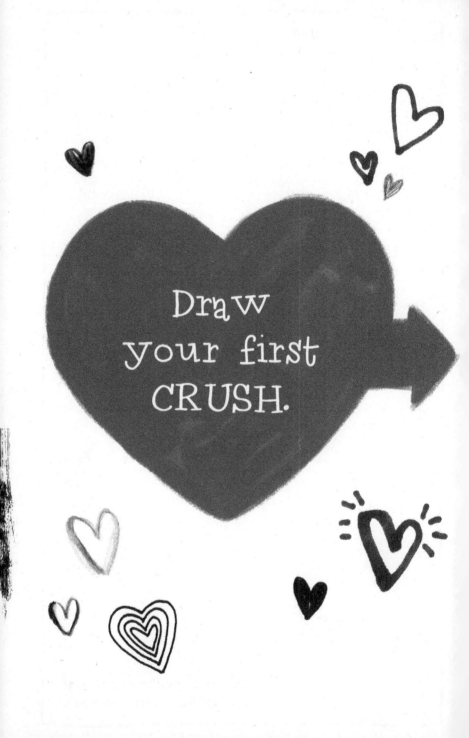

Draw
your first
CRUSH.

WRITE THEIR NAME IN CODE.

_____

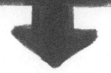

Who was your
favourite teacher
ever? Draw them.

**Just the best of a bad bunch,
or were they a real inspiration?**

DRAW A PICTURE OF YOUR FAVOURITE CHARACTER FROM A BOOK, TV PROGRAMME OR VIDEO GAME.

What made them awesome?

What was the first single/album you bought? Draw the cover art here.

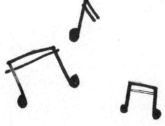

Still proud of your choice...?

Draw yourself on the best day trip you've ever had.

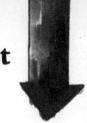

DESCRIBE THE WHOLE THING.

Draw a picture of the escapade that got you in the biggest trouble at school (even if it wasn't even your fault!)

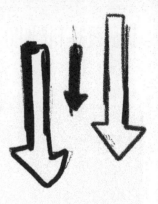

WRITE YOUR PUNISHMENT HERE.

DRAW YOUR FIRST KISS (EVEN IF IT WAS REALLY SLOPPY).

WRITE THE STORY AS THOUGH IT'S A ROMANCE NOVEL.

Draw yourself in a P.E. lesson.

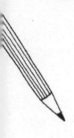

Did you love it, or HATE it?

DRAW YOUR 'COOLEST' OUTFIT ON NON-UNIFORM DAY.

Describe how your sartorial tastes have changed since then.

_____
_____
_____
_____
_____
_____
_____
_____
_____
_____
_____
_____
_____
_____
_____
_____
_____
_____
_____

Illustrate your favourite subject at school.

Why did you like it?

Draw your first
proper boyfriend
or girlfriend
(or your ideal
one if you don't
have one yet).

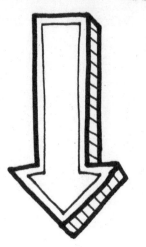

LIST ALL THEIR BEST AND WORST QUALITIES.

BEST	WORST

Draw the most wild night out you've ever been on.

Tell the whole story - if there are any gaps in your memory, ask a friend.

DRAW THE THING YOU DID THAT YOU'RE MOST ASHAMED OF.

Why did you do it??

DRAW YOUR FAVOURITE FANCY-DRESS OUTFIT EVER.

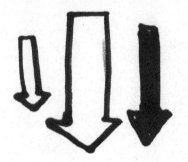

Describe the party you wore it to.

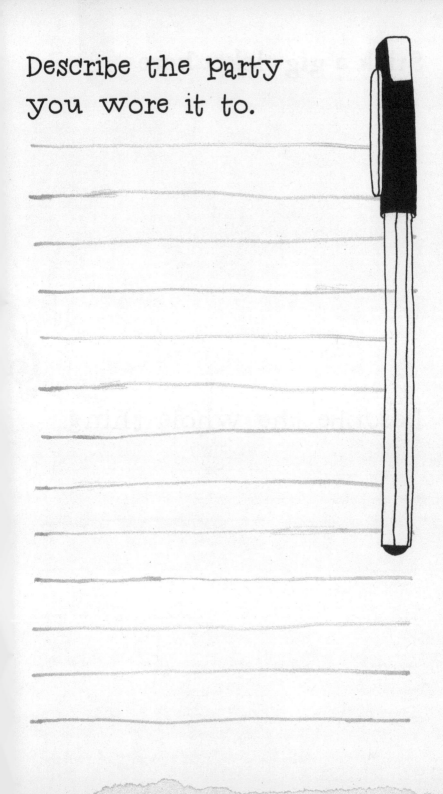

Stick a gig ticket here

Describe the whole thing.

_____

_____

_____

_____

_____

_____

_____

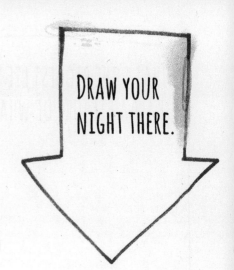

DRAW YOUR
NIGHT THERE.

WHAT'S THE BIGGEST LIE YOU'VE EVER TOLD?
DRAW A PICTURE OF WHAT IT WAS ABOUT.

Why did you tell it?

Draw your first trip away with friends.

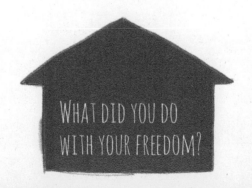

WHAT DID YOU DO
WITH YOUR FREEDOM?

Draw the house that most feels like home to you, even if you no longer live there.

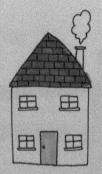

DESCRIBE IT AS THOUGH YOU'RE ON MTV CRIBS.

Draw the best
thing you've
ever done for
someone else.

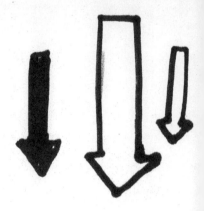

WHAT MADE YOU SO NOBLE?

Draw a cartoon strip for the story of you and your best friend, from the first time you met to the present day.

Dear ....

Write a letter to them about
what they mean to you.

DRAW YOUR FIRST
MOBILE PHONE.

What did you most
like to do with it?

Ring

Ring

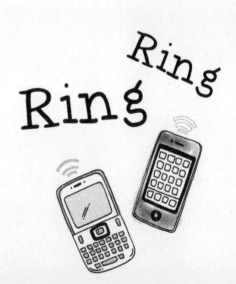

DRAW YOURSELF IN YOUR FIRST PAID JOB, EVEN IF IT WAS JUST A ONE-OFF.

DID YOU BOSS IT?

Draw your face the day you finished the hardest exams of your life.

What did you do to celebrate?

What's the most important thing you've ever learned? Draw the person who taught you.

WHAT WAS IT?

Draw your best
celebrity encounter.
Did you just DIE?

Tell the story - did you
embarrass yourself?

Illustrate the evolution of your hairstyle.

Describe each one in detail.
Especially the ones you hated.

What's your mum/dad's signature dish?

FIND OUT THE RECIPE AND WRITE IT HERE.

Draw the time
you felt on fleek.

How come you felt so awesome?

Draw the most
difficult thing
you've ever done.
(Well done you.)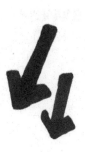

WHY WAS IT SO HARD?

Draw a picture of your family the last time you were all together, in the style of a Christmas card.

Describe the day - including any squabbles.

Draw the best
present you've
ever received.

WHY DID YOU
LOVE IT SO MUCH?

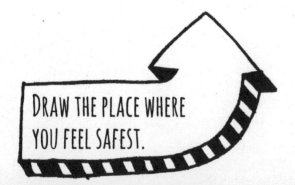

DRAW THE PLACE WHERE YOU FEEL SAFEST.

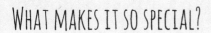

WHAT MAKES IT SO SPECIAL?

Draw your best ever dance moves -
anything from bopping up and down
as a baby to the cool shapes you
think you throw now.

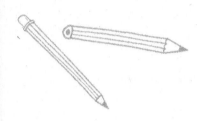

Describe each in detail.

Draw the most expensive thing you've ever bought.

Why did you buy it and was
it worth it?

Draw the time you seriously threw some shade.

How great did that feel?

Complete this storyboard for a dream or nightmare you had, that you'll never forget...

Get one of your friends to draw a picture of you, write the date and sign it.

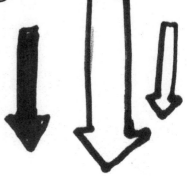

ASK THEM TO LIST FIVE REASONS WHY YOU'RE FRIENDS HERE:

1.

2.

3.

4.

5.

Draw what you look like when you cry (red cheeks, veins popping, swollen eyes - the works).

WHY DID YOU LAST CRY?

Draw the most dangerous thing you've ever done.

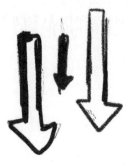

What made you do it??

Draw the person
or thing that broke
your heart.

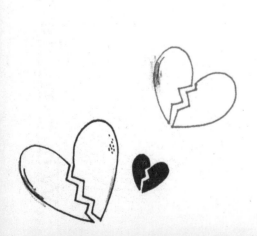

Write them a letter that you'll never send.

Draw yourself with a lightbulb over your head.

WRITE THE BEST IDEA YOU'VE EVER HAD – FOR A BUSINESS, A BOOK, TO CHANGE THE WORLD...

Draw the cover of your autobiography.

WRITE THE BACK COVER BLURB.

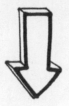

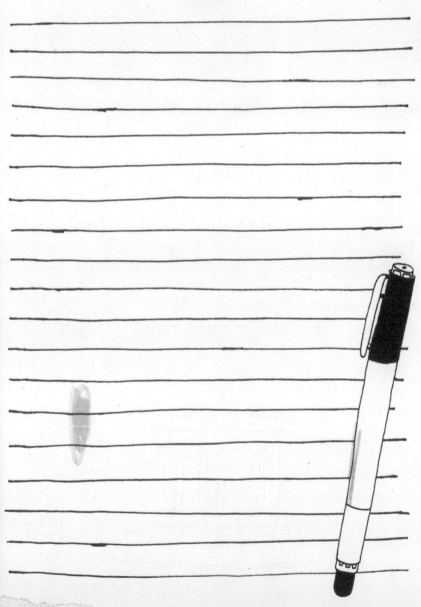

DRAW YOURSELF ON TOP
OF THIS PODIUM.

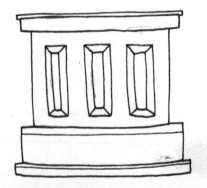

WRITE DOWN A LIST OF THINGS YOU'RE PROUD OF. PUT
THIS PAGE IN YOUR BEDROOM SO YOU'LL SEE IT EVERY DAY.

Draw the person you've most disliked in your life falling off a cliff.

WHY DID YOU HATE THEM SO MUCH?

Draw a picture for someone you need to say sorry to, rip it out and give it to them.

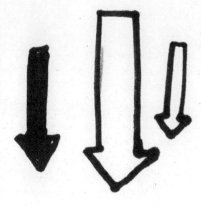

FINISH THIS SENTENCE: I'M SORRY THAT I ...

Draw the person
you miss the most.

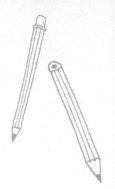

What do you wish you could say to them?

DRAW A PROTEST BANNER ABOUT
SOMETHING THAT YOU CARE ABOUT.

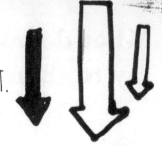

Write down why this is important to you.

Draw a Pinterest-style board of your favourite things

Which would you take to a desert island and why?

Face your fears, and draw the thing you're most scared of.

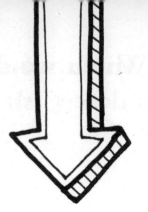

Why does it get to you? ⌒↗

Draw your favourite
daydream (with
your eyes closed).

Explain your design.

Draw yourself as a superhero!

WHAT POWERS (BOTH REAL AND IMAGINARY) WOULD YOU HAVE?

Invent a new emoji
that sums you up.

Why this one? ⬆

LIST ALL THE THINGS YOU LIKE ABOUT YOUR APPEARANCE (NO NEGATIVES ALLOWED).

_____

_____

_____

_____

_____

_____

_____

_____

Draw a selfie and take a picture of it.

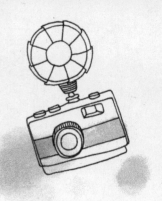

Draw yourself on your wedding day (either as it was, or how you imagine it will be).

Describe the day.

Draw the place you'd most like to go in the world, with the person you'd like to go with.

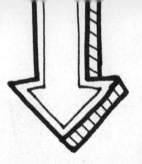

EXPLAIN WHY.

DRAW YOUR THOUGHTFUL FACE.

Write a letter to your past self about
what you wish you'd known then.

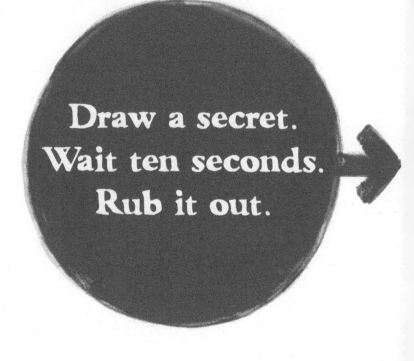

Draw a secret.
Wait ten seconds.
Rub it out.

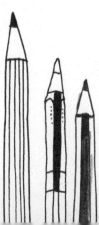

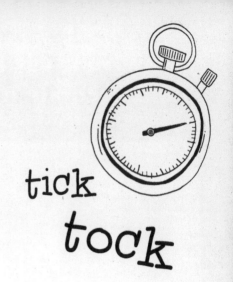

tick

tock

Draw your age here (and decorate it nicely).

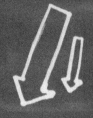

Write down the most important event in each year of your life.

_____

_____

_____

_____

_____

_____

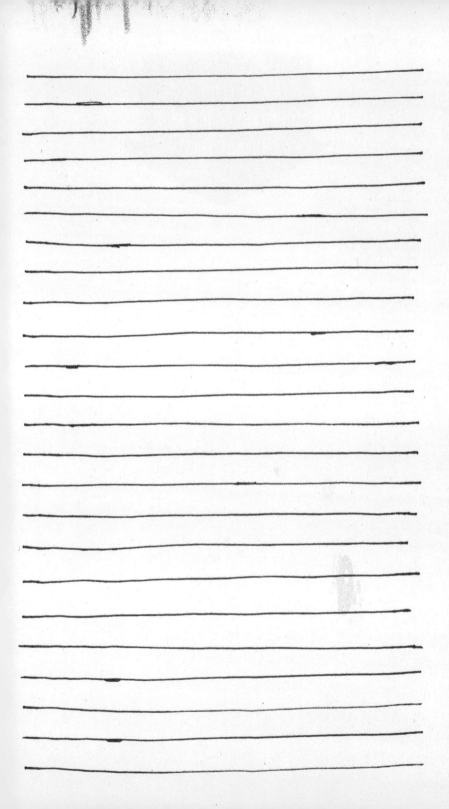

DRAW THE FIRST THING
YOU'D BUY IF YOU WON
THE LOTTERY.

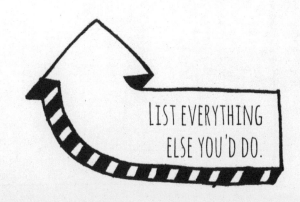

List everything else you'd do.

CURRENT MOOD:

_____

YOUR FACE:

Explain why you're feeling that way.

_____

_____

_____

_____

_____

_____

_____

_____

_____

_____

_____

_____

Complete this A-Z of YOU.

A ....   B ....

E ....   F ....

I ....   J ....

M ....   N ....

Q ....   R ....

U ....   V ....

Y ....   Z ....

C .... D ....

G .... H ....

K .... L ....

O .... P ....

S .... T ....

W .... X ....

DRAW WHAT HAS BEEN THE MOST IMPORTANT, AMAZING OR
LIFE-CHANGING THING TO HAPPEN IN YOUR LIFE SO FAR.

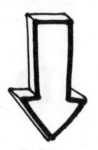

Describe it.

This is the very important LAST DRAWING. Close your eyes, think of a memory you haven't drawn so far in this book... You know what to do.

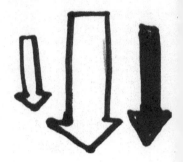

When you have
completed this
book, decorate
this tick however
you like.

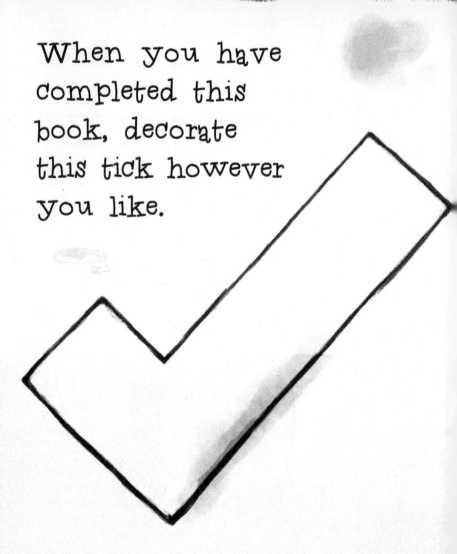

Now that you have drawn your
life so far, go out there and make
more memories...